Beats of Thought

Rupinder Kaur Kaiche

PARTRIDGE

To order additional copies of this book, contact
Partridge India
000 800 10062 62
orders.india@partridgepublishing.com

www.partridgepublishing.com/india

CONTENTS

Acknowledgement

My deepest gratitude to all the wonderful people who have touched my life and been an inspiration to me.

My special thanks to my wonderful daughter Aditri, without whose inputs this book would not have been possible. I would like to thank my very supportive husband Rahul, who also happens to be my best critic along with my son Karan. Their support and suggestions are invaluable to me.

My deepest thanks to my mother, Balwant Kaur, who initiated me into this beautiful world of poetry and has been my pillar of support all these years.

A fond remembrance of my father, Ranjit Singh, who inculcated in me the vision to appreciate beauty in simplest of things.

My special thanks to all my family and friends.

This book is dedicated
to the treasured memory of my late father
Ranjit Singh
To the cherished support of my mother, Balwant Kaur, husband,
Rahul, Karan
and Aditri.

Foreword

'Let me not be so busy
     Listening to music,
That I miss the
     Bird chirping on my sill,
Let me not be so comfortable
     Within the warmth of my walls,
That I miss the
     Fresh breeze outside,
Let me not be so glued
     To the technology at hand,
That I miss the
     intricacies of nature around.'

In today's world, where we are all busy trying to walk the extra mile to achieve our targets of success, we loose out on real happiness. The little lily flower fresh abloom, the first shower of rain, the bright sunshine, the gentle tickling wind, the humble bowing tree are the sights we tend to miss frequently for the hours spent in front of gadgets. We are losing out on happiness, peace and tranquility that nature offers us in abundance.

Let us all stop for a minute each day to look outside our windows, to look above at the vast sky, to appreciate the fragrance of the fresh flower, to feel the wind in our hair, to listen to the song of the cuckoo and sing along in happiness. Let us all open our hearts to take in the refreshing beauty of nature and work together towards preserving it. Let us make our planet beautiful and safe for all.

My poems are a reflection of my thoughts.

Beats of Thought

Like wild stallions in virgin land,
Unbridled race my thoughts.
Fine 'n' intricate as grains of sand,
How could have I fought?

Sometimes pleasant like a fragrant rose,
Sometimes lava of volcanic erruption.
Entangled like a mesh of foes,
Oh! wildfire out for combustion.

When at peace, world's at my feet,
Positivity abounds, happiness around,
Knowledge abounds, when upbeat.
Beats of thought . . . all kinds of sound!

Ink on the Pages

The ink that falls on expressionless paper,
From the exquisite hands of the fine painter,
The dream in his eyes deep crater,
Fall naked as an inventive entertainer.

He is the lord magician,
To transform with his deft fingers,
A humble ink into art bewitching,
Into forms, as the colours intermingle.

The ink that rides the hypnotic pen,
Of the captivating musician,
A peep into the poet's heavenly den,
Ah! intoxicating world of adroitness.

The firm ink that fills the pages,
Of books that lead the world,
The astute scientist, witted statesmen, insightful sages,
The ink that speaks many words.

Broken Shoe

Miles to walk,
Through the dungeons,
The caves, the crevices,
Of my shattered mind.

  As I get up after a fall,
  Clutching my fears close to my chest,
  My heart plummets the depths,
  Of darkness of my petrified mind.

Finding my way nervously,
Thru' the meandering maze,
I find the other half of my broken shoe,
As the clouds leave my mind fearless.

The mist of joy

In the cloud of mist,
Lay droplets of joy,
They settled on me,
That I jumped to toy.

Drenched was I,
Eyes clouded till brim,
Yet my arms outstretched,
To engulf the cloud slim!

You are my Rock

Two small eyes opened,
Blinded with worldly confusion.
Your massive hands . . . .,
Shaded me to a clear vision.

Two small feet fumbled,
The path was winding n rocky.
Your firm hands . . . .,
Held me till safety.

Two small hands grew,
From tender to rough.
Yet they searched for a pat . . .,
Of hands aging, fragile yet tough.

Somewhere along my walk,
Your hands left me . . . sad,
Yet I seek heavens for that rock!
You were for me my Dad.

The rumbling laughter

The roar of thunder,
Settled on leaf tender,
Only to slip hereafter,
With the rumbling of laughter.

The lightning that clashed,
Brightness on horizon splashed,
Danced on cheeks brighter,
With the rumbling of laughter.

Down poured the flooding rains,
Submerging all gains,
Drowned by a tear slighter,
With the rumbling of laughter.

The whispering leaves

The whispering leaves,
The drumming sheep,
Of dancing bamboos,
Over snails asleep.

Let your song glide,
Ride high over tide,
Tickle the shimmering waters,
Over the horizon slide.

When your words dance,
Under the moon's glance,
With the croaking frogs,
And peace enhance.

There we shall meet,
My dancing words shall greet,
Oh! My divine friend,
My world at your feet.

Universe in my arms

I am a floating gel,
As I merge with outer plasma,
You see me a beautiful women,
I see you my extension of yesterday,
I breathe the air,
and the air I become,
free, drifting, sailing 'n' soaring,
And the air augments me,
I behold the universe,
Spectacular, stupendous, ginormous,
It empowers my extended arms 'n' mingles,
In me lies the universe.

Let the winds blow

Let the winds blow
Strong and freezing,
Let them shake the core
Of my very being.

Let my soul rise
From slumber of darkness,
Into a ray bright 'n' fine
And shower peace and happiness.

Let me be the hand that shakes
The misery and evil away,
Let such wind blow that takes
The last tear far away.

Let the winds of change
Touch every heart a tender,
Oh! Lord thy love such arrange
Unto each other we surrender.

Light a candle

Light a candle my son,
In memory of love,
For it died long unsung,
Cheating men did shove.

      Light a candle my son,
      In memory of peace,
      Men fight daggers 'n' gun,
      Nations conflict doesn't cease.

Light a candle my son,
In memory of nature,
Dying tigers burning trees a ton,
Turtles, sparrows, snakes ah! Endanger.

      Light a candle my son,
      In memory of earth,
      For how long will it undone,
      Hatred, anger ah! No dearth.

Daughter of an army officer

I woke up in the morning to a siren's blow,
Was it war or peace was hard to know,
Then I realized it was wake up slaughterer,
Yet no worries for the daughter of an Army officer.

Miles were we from the bustling crowd,
Nestled amidst wooded hills proud,
With echoes of regular gun shots lost among conifer,
Stood tall the daughter of an Army officer.

Laughter was loud 'n' hearty whenever could,
For a fear lurked of unhappy news should,
"Goodbyes", in the morning were heart softener,
Tearless 'n' proud stood the daughter of an Army officer.

Dancing words

Sing O! dear
Sing loud 'n' clear,
Sing to the mountains
Far and near.

Let your melody quiver,
Jump over river,
Step on the wind,
And on the cloud shimmer.

The splashing waves of wonder,
The rumbling thunder,
The sparkling lightning,
Ah! soul surrender.

The pitter patter dripping,
Oh! The raindrops falling,
The tinkling of pebbles,
Dancing and slipping.

The Hand that carved the world

The zesty exuberance of His creation,
The undying flow of ardent passion,
Awe-struck by His magnificance,
By the hand that carved the world.

The fluid flow of boundless energy,
The agile ease of sauve creativity,
Millions of forms, each in synergy,
Ah! the hand that carved the world.

The mesmerizing intercourse of emotions,
Calm silence of angelic love, unalloyed anger,
Distressing fear, messianic trust'n'anticipation,
Oh! the hand that carved the world.

Raging fire

The raging fire,
My heart's desire.
A morsel of food,
For my stomach nude.
A hand of paul,
To wipe a tear drop fall.

The raging fire,
A mind so tire.
A smile to flatter,
For a soul in tatter.
Some mercy of humanity,
To live with dignity.

Music of silence

In the depths of darkness
A star tinkles,
It's light dances
In silence mingles.

In the depths of darkness
A cloud moans,
As the wind salsas
In harmony it soars.

In the depths of darkness
Echoes the laughter,
Of the waves naughtiness
With the sea gulls flutter.

In the depths of darkness
Floats the fragrance high,
The song of heavens
To the music of silence.

Ladybird

A royal princess,
Or is it an elegant lady,
An enchanting temptress,
Ah! A sauve haydee.

    With a nubile frame,
    And petite, brisk wings,
    Oh! You bewitching dame!
    Tranquility with it she brings.

Bright orange or deep red,
And perfect black dots,
To the fore a profound head,
The ladybird, a heavenly queen consort.

Be A Man

Shouting, abusing, unkind words,
Are not powerful as you feel,
Don't assume to be a man of sword,
To clinche your final deal.

Ramble not with an air of extravagance,
For many swagger and fall prey,
Rise with dignity, savour ampleness,
Be a man of your word, pray!

Tall of compassion and character dear,
With the strength of love and faith,
May you defeat all pain and fear,
Gentle and trustworthy a man, let all saith.

The Lost Melody

Holding dad's strong hands,
Out for a stroll in the woods.
We were greeted by the buzzying..,
Dradonflies hovering over our heads.
The screeching of the monkeys,
As they scaled the tree tops,
Only to jump on the vine of another.
As the larks began to warble,
Fluttering away from squealing mice,
Finding their way over rustling dry leaves.
Squeaking runs the hare,
Being chased by snorting boars.
Amidst this the distant laugh of hyenas.,
Mesmerized we stood as the wind purred past.
Chirring hopped the grasshoppers,
From one shrub to another.
With fear paralysed we stood..,
Hearing the far trumpet.
Whispering comfort in my ears,
Dad pointed to the humming bees,
And the butterflies sucking the nectar away.
Behind the trees peeped two eyes,
Above a branching network of antlers.
As the grunting deers fled away,
We walked back home;
Leaving the whimpering bats behind,
And the chirping cricket welcoming the night.
As I take my son to the jungle,
To look for familiar sounds, years later,
I am aghast! Searching for the lost melody.

Don't wait for me

The waves are singing,
To the sea gulls dance.
Dolphins playing . . . . . .
Wind steals a glance.

The sky bends down
To plant a kiss,
As the rain pours around,
With the sun amiss.

Don't wait for me,
I'm lost in the sky.
Or is it the sea
That's flown me high?

Daughter of a lesser God

'You'll tell me whom to pray,
    In your myriad of rituals and ways,
To each a different word,
    Am I not free to seek my God?

I toiled day 'n' night, just as you;
    And sleepless nights just to be 'Me',
Yet you teach me 'pray to who',
    Am I daughter of a lesser God?

A man or just a soul, O! Lord,
   Have I not birthed The Divine?
Let me be of a lesser God,
   But let my God be mine!!

Love..to find Him

It's hard to feel Him in me,
Harder to see Him in you,
Can I perceive Him in my enemy?
The millions that walk thru'.

When I step on a helpless insect,
Why can I not sense Him?
Why can I not from a butcher protect?
The beings whose survival is grim.

When will I sense him all around?
Close my eyes or with open ones,
Discern the love he showers abound,
Love all boundlessly.....you'll find Him.

O! Woman

Let your charm
       Sway people off their feet,
Let your love
       Be abundant, genuine 'n' sweet,
Let your smile honey,
       Wash away all pain,
Let your imperturbable eyes
       Bring empathy 'n' warmth like a hurricane,
Let your assertive hands rise
       Always to care and cure,
Let your feet walk an extra mile
       For your principles 'n' dignity so sure,
Let not anyone instill fear
       For you are confidence personified,
You are the nurturer
       Who takes the world along in your stride,
May you be the woman
       To change the face of humanity,
You, with your tender hands
       Give hope 'n' strength to your intellectuality.'

Happiness unclinched

Talk to the little flower,
Sitting snuggly amidst ravishing greens,
Its exuberant colour, its carefree demure,
Drenched in happiness unclinched!!a queen.

Look at the spirited butterfly alluring,
As it coyly glides over flowers blooming,
With a dash of pink, blue 'n' orange on wings fluttering,
Splashing happiness unclinched, grooming.

Feel the tickling love of the grass,
As it gives your feet a cushioned massage,
All luxury, comfort 'n' love, it surpass,
Oozing happiness unclinched, surcharge.

Chill! Mom

Chill mom!! I often hear unkind,
As I attempt to open my mouth,
Did telepathic conversation cross their mind?
Getting rejected by contemporary youth.

To arouse them out of slumber,
Walk the way instead of motor,
Amidst the cacophony of gadgetic blunder,
Your words fall prey to strategic emoter.

With diverse healthy food on table,
Their squirmish face spills the beans,
Discipline is ancient as horses fables,
Chill mom!! They're your genes!

Give me back

Sitting sad a sparrow on the dry twig,
Of a tree shorn its life.
Am I free or in a brig?
No food on trees, how to survive?

      With prying bright hunter's eyes,
      Roams the leopard for a prey.
      Large barren land, no jungle it cries,
      Piercing through city houses astray.

Struggling to walk under scorching sun,
A herd of dear panting for water.
A school of fish grappling for air,
Drowning in a sea full of scum!

      Give me back O!man my world serene,
      Coolness of the dense forest.,
      Sweetness of the cool water clean,
      My food, my peace, my life.

A Cell

A tiny little cell,
     Not visible to you 'n' me,
Yet a world in itself,
     That's the life in you 'n' me.

It eats, it breathes,
     It makes, it breaks,
The universe in itself it completes,
     Haemostasis it always maintains.

It's enegy so full 'n' fluid,
     That's you today, me tomorrow.
The power of the mind; undisputed,
     The heartbeat; its joy 'n 'sorrow.

Lost Simplicity

The days are long and deceitful,
The nights dishonest and cunning,
The weather is like a camelion lethal,
Winds run amok fuming.

So are men and women today,
A whirlwind of cocktail emotions,
With a smile they poke a jibe shoddy,
And pollute the beautiful creation.

Wicked and nasty like crawling worms,
Spreading tentacles of hatred and acidity,
Drenched under the toxic rain they squirm,
Long lost are the days of simplicity.

Give Me My Wings

I fly for miles over barren land,
To look for the tree who'll house me,
Under the burning sun over rancid sand,
Searching for a lone cloud who'll quench me.

Tall buildings, all concrete, I've lost ground,
Meandering thru' buzzing planes searching the sky,
Not a water to splash, scum a pound,
Give me my wings, I'm lost to fly.

Anger......

Do not O!man belittle me,
Cover not your weaknesses with me.
I am energy, I am power,
I can fulfill your heart's desire.

Do not suppress when I ride inside,
Make me a weapon of justice denied,
Give me a voice that echoes change,
From violence 'n' hatred become estrange.

Grow with me as I snowball,
Determined to love, stand tall,
Let your mind to peace adhere,
You stand without fear 'n' I shall dissapear.

The Catterpillar in the box

Plop falls the catterpillar in the box,
Dropped by two fingers hastily,
With inquisitive eyes engulfing each block,
As the catterpillar strolls steathily.

Caught and claustrophobic it feels,
Struggling over slippery, barren floor,
Sequestered away from the green fields,
The birds, the bees, insects . . .forlorn.

The little boy fed his friend dearly,
Waiting for a lifetime of friendship,
One morning flew out a moth merrily,
To freedom!! Confinement outstrip.

Old School

Behind those tall walls,
Echoes a carefree laughter,
The breezy brush with books,
And the heated discussion's aftermath.
To unworried exams of sorts,
And the relaxed smiles of teachers.

On those hard wooden chairs,
Are imprinted the cherished memories,
Of teachings virtous and valuable,
Which help me stand tall,
In a world of ruthless aggression
And paint my own bust.

The long sunny corridors,
Are reminance of bubbly chitchats,
Friends and foes, makes and breaks,
Of future plans and present strategies,
Classes missed, punishments withstood,
Of football played and combats avoided.

Dusk

The hustle and bustle,
A moment ago,
Has lost it's way,
Amidst the calmness so.

> The crimson sky,
> And the green around,
> The quiet birds . . .,
> Saying "don't make a sound".

The closing petals,
Of the weary flowers,
The humming bees,
Settle after tiring hours.

> The shimmering waters,
> Of the golden river,
> A shadow floating,
> Enjoying the serene calm river.

Far away in the burning fields,
A humble soul seperating husk,
Oh! what beauty God has showered,
At this time of dusk.

Come June

My eyes are tired squinting . . . .,
Awaiting your esteemed arrival,
the dark laden clouds gathering,
Come June, you mean survival.

The earth is parched, as my lips,
Looking wishfully to heavens for respite,
Deliver me from the fear of apocalypse.
Come June, forgive my despite.

Rivers are dry, no crops survive,
Without rain, how am I to sustain?
My greed fed this, crisis I'd contrive,
Come June, bring me some rain.

Don't dust me away

Don't dust me away,
For I'll come back stronger,
Maybe I'm not ripe today,
I'll not make you wait longer.

    The gravelled path might hurt,
    But I carry a basket of flowers,
    The days might get short,
    My vision will be clear inspite the shower.

You may leave me alone,
But my lord will not abandon,
Don't dust me away so soon,
Look for the star on the horizon.

The dance of the devil

We cut, we burn, we uproot,
No love, no respect, no compassion,
How many are we to mute,
Before the dance of the devil we see.

We leave no branches for the birds,
Homeless they fly under scorching heat,
No jungles for the destitute animal herds,
How long to the dance of the devil we concede.

My heart

Singing in the midst of storm,
Laughing after a mighty fall,
Standing up after a disaster tall,
My heart has done it all.

Dancing with the falling rain,
Beating to the cuckoos gain,
Galloping over valleys 'n' plains,
My heart has happiness gain.

Splashing the rainbow of love,
With blessings pouring from above,
Laughter does anger shove,
My heart is serene like a dove.

Over a cup of coffee

The first rays of sun thru' the window,
The cuckoo giving the wake-up call,
The fresh aroma of coffee glides over the pillow,
To a cup of coffee I'm in thrall.

Meetings over long tables,
Big discussions, bigger decisions,
A cup of coffee to overcome the babel,
And take charge with precision.

Moms meet over a cup of coffee,
Deciding what dinner table should host,
The children's best book and hobby,
What makes the men toast!

Over a cup of coffee, friends meet,
After a long day of work 'n' stress,
A little laughter, with a clap they greet,
And lo! To take on life all afresh.

A Pot

Round 'n' round goes the potter's wheels,
Blissful in its rhythmic dance,
Oblivious to the potter at heel,
Who struggles to take its chance.

Wet mud that sits on his hand,
Goes up and down to fall,
Only to be pulled up the stand,
Makes it feel so small.

He breaks and rebreaks it all,
Till it dances to the same tune,
And lo! Behold stands a pot tall,
A marvel to cherish all noon.

And as the piercing sun rays,
Matures it into a cool pot,
It gives sweet chilled waters on hot days,
An elixir to a life besot.

Light or Fantasy

Skyscrapers will eat away the jungles,
Trees will grow on walls,
But where will the animals snuggle,
And where will you go for a walk?

Maze of streets will cover the earth,
Ships will invade the rivers 'n' seas,
And where would the fish swim in mirth,
You get drinking water clean?

Rays of different frequencies width,
Will occupy all layers of atmosphere,
And where would the birds 'n' insects berth,
You get your precious peace?

The mirror is loud and clear

Sparkling water gushed down,
The peaks laden with snow so pure,
Breaking the hardened ice crown,
Meandering thru' rocks so demure.

    Engorged with joy, frolic 'n' impishness,
    Till it reaches cities so prosperous,
    They bleed it, filling with trash scourings,
    Exhausted, struggling it seeks the sea.

With opulence, has vanished fear,
In comfort and gratification you sway,
But the mirror is loud 'n' clear,
See O!man your life drowning away

Ah! Guru

You are the life force in me,
The nurturer of my soul,
You blessed me to be me,
Else would've been a worthless mole.

You blessed me immense,
And made my place in this world,
You taught me life essence,
And saved me from being tortured.

Pray grace me with your love,
That I may share with all,
Endow me to sing Wah Guru 'n' rise above,
That which impresses you.

Dancing Earth

The supple spin
      And the day turns night.
The scorching heat
      Is overpowered by serene peace.

The elegant walk
      Around the alluring sun,
And the chilly nip in the air
      Tickling the daffodils.

As the jungle echoes
      To the jig of the wind,
The cosmos twirls
      To the dancing earth.

Technology don't dare

Now that you gave me cars,
Don't dare to make me forget walking,
Your high speed trains bizarre,
When will I try running?

From sturdy handsets to swanky mobiles,
Sophisticated earplugs to keep me glued,
I forgot my neighbours, chatted across miles,
What attitude did I exude!

Computers and machines to work for me,
Mental 'n' physical work all done,
You're making my brain'n'muscles dissappear,
Rule over me when I'm outdone.

I improvised for my aid,
So I could progress leaps'n' bounds,
But technology don't dare,
You will hear my commands resound.

I'm Busy

I'm busy . . .,
Drowning in the ocean of dissonance,
Yet I search for waves of quietude.

I'm busy . . .,
Smiling for a sea of faces,
Yet I long for love in atleast one!

I'm busy . . .,
Slogging to give comfort to children,
But I missed seeing their tiny steps.

I'm busy . . .,
Toiling to spread happiness,
And oh! I forgot to smile.

I'm busy . . .,
Why am I so busy, O! Lord,
If I can't stop to feel you all around.

A Painting on the Wall

The little girl on the bike,
Struggling to ride it straight.
Two ponytails hanging each side,
Sharp eyes challanging her fate.

Tired from the days ride,
Muddy sweat trickling down cheeks soft,
Onto the cozy bed she slides,
After a soothing wash with water hot.

Drowned in the sea of dreams,
She floats on the cloud of colours,
Lighting her alley falls a sun beam,
Brightning the horizon that was duller.

With graceful strokes on canvas white,
Stands a woman with a candle slight,
Falling behind her the shadow so might,
Her face soft, humble and bright.

And then rose the sun amidst sky blue,
The melodious voice of mother to call,
With eyes opening to the day anew,
Was "the Painting on the wall".

Living with a Stranger

Young and beautiful,
With dreams floating,
I danced my way,
Into the arms of a stranger.

      I followed him like a shadow,
      Silently running to keep pace,
      Half way thru' the journey . . .,
      I forgot to talk, he to recognise my face.

We walked, we ran,
We stumbled, we fell,
We cried to the world for a hand,
But forgot to hold each other!

Flames of fire

The flames of fire all around,
Ravaging the precious peace to null,
Despair, helplessness so profound,
Let them not engulf all.

Sound of guns firing fill the air,
The stench of dead irrepressible,
Cities vanquished by flames of fire,
Let it not become insuppressible.

Hunger paralyses old and young,
Eyes dried of tears flash agony,
Flames of fire burn the stomach unsung,
Let it not incinerate the soul brutally.

Spice of Life

The tiny hands which held you tight,
Are now lifted to say goodbye,
You cajoled them to agree, now they decide,
Change is the spice of life.

        The handsome hunk you fell in love,
        And fought with the world hand in glove,
        Is lost to you for the worldly strife,
        Change is the spice of life.

You were bright and beautiful,
Strong-willed, naughty and musical,
Peaceful 'n' sturdy to face the world you strive,
Change is the spice of life.

Sunset

In the ocean of red,
Are the waves of yellow,
Boats of maroon,
And their oars are black.

The ocean is calm,
Yet the waves violent,
The boats are still,
With the oars in motion.

This immense beauty is not,
A painter's masterpeice, a poet's dream,
Its the sunset sky, loaded with clouds,
And the birds sailing past .

Lightning Source UK Ltd.
Milton Keynes UK
UKHW011520080321
379988UK00002B/355